HEART POETRY!

**Dedicated to my kid sister
"untie"**

TABLE OF CONTENTS

ACHING SOUL

My soul ,aches
Aches, for anything
Something, everything

That may ,clam it

Something, it thinks it
knows
Anything , it can't choose
Everything , it can't get
Something, anything,
everything special

Special, like peace
Rare , like true love
Often ,like oxygen
Usual, like unemployment

My soul ,aches
Aches ,for anything
Something, everything
That may ,clam it

Peace ,we all need
True love, we all chase
Oxygen, we can't do
without
Unemployment, to
eradicate

Aching soul, stops aching
True love , is found

Oxygen, is plentiful
Unemployment, to
employment

Aching soul ,is happy
As happy , as toddler
A toddler, to new weds
New weds , during
honeymoon

My soul ,aches
Aches ,for anything

Something, everything
That may ,clam it

New weds , in a new house
A new house, gifted
Gifted ,by the loved ones
Loved ones, generosity

Generosity, so rare
As rare , as tree
Trees , replaced by concrete

Concrete ,everywhere

Everywhere, modernity
Modernity , replacing
Replacing , everything
Everything , anything

My soul ,aches
Aches ,for anything
Something, everything
That may ,clam it

LOST STRANGER

Lost stranger , roams
Roams, around
Looking ,for something
Anything, everything

Everything, that brings him
happiness
Happiness, that's very
elusive
As elusive, as money
Money , that buys
happiness

Lost stranger , is a loner
Running away , from
himself
Keeping , all thoughts to
himself
Thoughts about, something

Something, that's so elusive
As elusive, as happiness
As rare , as rare as trust
Trust , can't be bought

Lost stranger , roams
Roams, around
Looking ,for something
Anything, everything

Lost stranger, talks
Talks , about the past
Glorious , like Spartacus
Torturous, like slavery

The past , that haunts
Haunts, his soul
His spirit, unsettled
Unsettled, like a heartthrob
A past ,he tries to settle

A soul ,he tries to clam
A spirit , so stubborn
As stubborn , as goat

Lost stranger , roams
Roams, around
Looking ,for something
Anything, everything

Lost stranger, talks
Talks , about the past
Glorious , like Spartacus
Torturous, like slavery

Lost stranger ,wants love

Lost stranger, wants success
Lost stranger, wants a home
A home , not a house
Lost stranger , roams
Roams, around
Looking ,for something
Anything, everything

A home ,he will share
A home , full of love
A home , full of peace
A home , with loved ones

Loved ones ,he ran from
Loved ones , that haunt him
Loved ones , he misses
Loved ones , he really needs

Lost stranger, needs
He needs , something he
didn't treasure
Something ,he can get back
Something , money can't
buy

Lost stranger , roams
Roams, around
Looking ,for something
Anything, everything

3.LIFE

Life , so mysterious
Mysterious, like the night
The night , dark without
stars
As dark , as the night

Life , so hopeless
As hopeless , as chasing
one's shadow
A shadow , so elusive
Elusive, especially at night

Life , so hopeful

As hopeful, as a political
aspirant
Aspiring, to win an election
An election, so mysterious
like the dark

Life , so blissful
As blissful, as a blooming
flower
A flower , blooming in
summer
Summer, so beautiful
As beautiful, as the flower

Life , so hateful
As hateful , as religion
Religion, used to divide
Division, instead of unity

Life , so miserable
As miserable, as a job
seeker
A job seeker , without a
godfather
A godfather, to grease
hands

Life , so precious
As precious, as life
Life ,a gift from God
God , whose merciful

Life , so disgusting
As disgusting, as racism
Racism, practiced by racists
Racists ,who are ignorant

Life , so hopeful
As hopeful, as a new
employee

An employee, who badly
needed a brake
A brake, after life put him
down

Life , so sweet
As sweet , as honey
Honey , from the bees
Bees , essential for life

Life , so great
As great , as victory

A victory, worked for
A victory, well deserved

Life ,so just
As just ,as God
Just , to a victim
A victim, to a survivor

Life , so gracious
As gracious , as saints
Saints , so rare
As rare , as honesty

4.SUCCESS

Success , what is it ?.

Success , how is it ?
Success ,when is it ?
Success , who gets it?

Success , comes
unexpectedly
So many think , it's easier
 As easier , as waking up
earlier
As earlier , as a mockingbird

Success , comes to those
who deserve it
But everyone, wants and
needs it

Why is it , so choosy
As choosy , as a vegetarian

Success , what is it ?.
Success , how is it ?
Success ,when is it ?
Success , who gets it?

Is happiness, success?
We all , want to be happy
But only, a few are real happy
The rest , we just live life as it is

Is love , success?
We all, want to beloved
By those , we love
But that's, not how it
usually happens

Is success , money ?
We all, want or need
money
But only, a few have money
Are they , more happy than
us ?

Success , what is it ?.

Success , how is it ?
Success ,when is it ?
Success , who gets it?

Is success, a family ?
We all, need a family
A family, filled with love
But only a few , have such
families

Is success, power?.
Power , to control others
Power ,to do as we want
without consequences

But we can't, tell because
only a few have such power
Success, who gets it ?

They say , those that
deserve it
But who ,knows who
deserves and doesn't
deserve it ?
Success, we all want it

Success , what is it ?.
Success , how is it ?
Success ,when is it ?
Success , who gets it?

Success , how does it show up ?
It shows up, like a house burglar
Unexpectedly , and unplanned for
But to only , those that deserve it

Success, calms us

Success, wipes the tears of
sleepless nights
Success, confirms our
doubts
Success , consoles our
restless self

Be successful ,as you might
Be careful , with success
As much as it sets you free
,it exposes the real you to
the world
A world, that needs a better
you

Success , what is it ?.
Success , how is it ?
Success ,when is it ?
Success , who gets it?

5.EDUCATION

Education , is sort after
Sort after ,by everyone
But few ,knows it's value
It's value ,can't be
quantified

Education, so mind enlightening
As enlightening, as a precious book
A precious book , with an ugly cover
No wonder they say , never judge a book by its cover

Education, so elusive
Elusive, to the unmotivated person
A person , who's lazy
Lazy ,to find out it's real value

Many claim, to be educated
Just because, they went to
school
But few ,understand the
difference
Between going to school ,
and being educated

Education, improves our
thinking
Education, makes us
understand one another
better

Education, should unite a society
Education, should enlighten the society

The society, should be educated
So as it will, make better plans
For future generations , and current generations
Plans , for prosperity and not doom

Education, should make us
equal
As equals , we should
reason
As equals, we should live
As equals, we should work

Education, should make us
better
Education, should make us
more understanding
Education, should make us
have empathy
Education, should unite us

Education, is the key to success
Success, so elusive
Even the educated, can't get it
Why is , education and success different?.

Education and success, very different
But share a similarity, both to elusive
Not only elusive , but also difficult

Difficult , to the
undetermined person

Undetermined person ,
gives up easily
But some might, be just
tired
Tired of ,the sleepless
nights
Sleepless nights, with no
success to show

Education, like a bright
lamp

Should be , used to light up society
A society, in need of answers
Answers , which are unanswered

Unanswered, by the past generations
Education , should make generations better

Better , in everything and
anything
That's why , education is
precious

6.A MAN'S AMBITIONS

Ambitions , like hope
Hope ,for a better day
A day ,we all impatiently wait for
Not knowing, when it will arrive

A man , without ambitions

Is like , a lawyer without the constitution
Ambitions , give the drive
A drive , to keep going

A man's ambitions, drive him
Like a vehicle, they drive
They drive him , to his desired future
A future, he must work for

Ambitions, so elusive

As elusive, as a person
owing you cash
Cash , that you lent in good
faith
For it is the faith , that
drives the ambitions

Ambitions, so great
As great , as he wants them
Ambitions, he controls
He either , makes it or
makes it

Everyman , deserves
ambitions

Ambitions, are like hope
A man without hope , is a
corpse
A corpse , moving around
like a zombie

A man , has to chase his
ambitions
Or live , to tell others how
ambitious he was
No one takes , stories
seriously compared to facts
Be ambitions, like you wish
to be

Ambitions, he keeps
guarded
Guarded, more than gold
As ambitions, can't be
quantified
He only , knows how
valuable they are

A man's ambitions, are his
personal dreams
Dreams ,of his boyhood
Now ,ready to chase them
So that , he can fulfill his
boyhood dreams

Dreams , aren't ambitions
Dreams , come and go
But ambitions, remain
constant
As constant , as racism in
the world

A man's ambitions, are his
own
He can choose, to share
them
Or keep them , locked deep
Deep into , his heart and
head

But ambitions , not fulfilled
Bring sorrow , to the man's
heart
A heart , healing from
failure

Failure, he can raise above
or that can kill his ambitions

Ambitions , to dangerous
Can destroy , a man
A man ,who isn't patient or
strategic
Be patient, if not strategic

7.HOME

Home , is it a house ?
Home , is it relatives ?
Home , is it a wife and kids
?
Home , is it precious?.

Home , is where the heart is
So they say , those who
think they know
They know too little, but
pretend to be masters

Masters of none , but
what's home ?.

Home , is a house
A house , not marvelous nor
expensive
A house , shared by loved
ones
A house , filled with warmth
and memories

Memories, so precious
More precious, than any precious stone
As precious stones, can be bought but not memories
Memories ,are lived and experienced

Home , is it a house ?
Home , is it relatives ?
Home , is it a wife and kids ?
Home , is it precious?.

Home , is relatives
Relative , who are precious
Relatives, who are around
Around ,during fortunes
and misfortunes

Fortunes , bring relatives
But misfortunes , prove
relatives
Relatives, don't need to be
by blood
Relatives, are by loyalty

As loyal , as a dog to its master
Always there , during sunny and rainy days
Always ready, to give a helping hand
A hand ,need anytime

Home, is it a house ?
Home , is it relatives ?
Home , is it a wife and kids ?
Home , is it precious?.

Home , is wife and kid
A wife ,so joyful and
hardworking
Her joy ,illuminated her
house like Venus
Kid , a blessing from God

God ,so precious and
faithful
That , He blesses and
protects
He protects, the family
A family, so precious

Kids , to carry on
To carry on , the family name
The family name , a guaranteed tree
A tree , blessed by God

Home, is it a house ?
Home , is it relatives ?
Home , is it a wife and kids ?
Home , is it precious?.

Home , is precious
They say , gold is precious
They say , diamonds are
precious
They have never , lost a
loved one

8.THE ROAD

The road ,to where ?

The road , we hate
The road , we love
Why are we , always on the road ?

The road , to where ?
To where , our legs takes us
Our legs , running away
Away , from pain

Pain ,take us on the road
Pain ,keep us on the road
Pain , makes us love the road
Pain , isn't the road

Why is pain , forcing us on
the road ?
Why can't we , face our
pains
Our pains , so painful
The road , tries to heal
them

The road ,to where ?
The road , we hate
The road , we love
Why are we , always on the
road ?

The road , we hate
We hate , but always on it
Like addicts ,we need it
We need it , to heal our
hurting souls

Souls ,hurt by the world
A world ,so hateful
A world, so inconsiderate
A world, we made

A world, forces us on the
road

On the road, within the
world
The same world ,that we
are running away from
The road , heals the hurting
soul

The road ,to where ?
The road , we hate
The road , we love
Why are we , always on the
road ?

The road ,we love

The road ,that takes us back
home
The road ,that leads us to
happiness
The road ,that leads us to
good health and success

The road , that takes us
home
Home ,where we belong
Home , to our loved ones
Our loved ones ,so precious

The road , that leads us to
happiness

Happiness, so rare
nowadays
More rare , than generosity
The road ,we all seek

The road , that leads us to
good health and success
Good health, so valuable
Success, so elusive
The road ,we all pray for

The road ,to where ?

The road , we hate
The road , we love
Why are we , always on the
road ?

9.THE FOREIGNER

The foreigner , always
wrong
The foreigner , always
hated
The foreigner , always
misunderstood
The foreigner, we all are

The foreigner , always
wrong
The assumption, we all
make
We make ,out of our
ignorance
Ignorance, so blissful

The assumption, we make
We make , because we
don't ask
We don't ask , because we
know better
We know better, so we
think

Our ignorance, so blissful
So blissful, that it makes us
blind
Blind ,to the obvious reality
Reality, so painful to admit

The foreigner , always
wrong
The foreigner , always
hated
The foreigner , always
misunderstood
The foreigner, we all are

The foreigner, always hated
Hated , for something
Hated , for anything
A foreigner, doesn't
understand

The foreigner, always hated
Hated , for trying to live
Hated , for searching better
things
Hated , for being human

The foreigner, doesn't
understand

Doesn't understand, the
hatred
Doesn't understand, the
stares and sneers
The foreigner, is human

The foreigner , always
wrong
The foreigner , always
hated
The foreigner , always
misunderstood
The foreigner, we all are

The foreigner, always
misunderstood
Misunderstood, for not
understanding the local
language
Misunderstood, why he
traveled this far
A foreigner, is human
A foreigner, is human
Human, chasing his dreams
Human , who needs help
Be humane , help a
foreigner

Human , chasing dreams

Dreams , take us to far
away lands
New lands , where we
become foreigners
New lands , we call home

he foreigner , always wrong
The foreigner , always
hated
The foreigner , always
misunderstood
The foreigner, we all are

10.LOVE

Love , what is it ?
Love , where is it ?
Love , who is it ?
Love , so elusive

Love , what is it
Love , is precious
Love , is patience
Love , is caring

Love , is precious

Precious, more than precious stones
Precious stones, have a price
A price , love doesn't have

Love , is patience
Patience, not common
Patience, a gift
A gift , not all have

Love , what is it ?
Love , where is it ?

Love , who is it ?
Love , so elusive

Love, where is it
Love , is everywhere ,
So they say ,but no one
knows
Where , exactly to get it

Everywhere , there is love
Love , is given
Love , isn't stolen or forced
on to
Love , is here and there
Love ,is given

Given ,by one to another
Love , is happiness
Happiness ,we all can give

Love , what is it ?
Love , where is it ?
Love , who is it ?
Love , so elusive

Love, who is it
Love , is anyone and
someone
Anyone, who treasures you
Someone , who values you
Anyone, who treasures you

Treasures you , enough to
accept your imperfections
Imperfections, in all of us
Perfections , we all love

Someone ,who values you
Values you , enough to be
help you
Help you ,to be a better
person

A better person, to love

Love , what is it ?
Love , where is it ?
Love , who is it ?
Love , so elusive

11. THE CITY

The city , we love
The city , dreams maker
The city , dreams wrecker

The city , so brutal

The city, we love
We love , the bright lights
We love , beautiful
skyscrapers
We love , the crowds

We love ,the bright lights
Soo bright , like our dreams
Our dreams, that brought
us to the city
The city , we will live in

We love , the crowds
Crowds , that show our
diversity
Crowds , of ambitions
Ambitions, that brought us
to the city

The city , we love
The city , dreams maker
The city , dreams wrecker
The city , so brutal

The city , dreams maker
Dreams , get us to the city

The city , has more
opportunities
Opportunities, for a better
tomorrow

The city , has more
opportunities
So they say ,until you get
into the city

More opportunities ,
becomes just another
phrase
A phrase , used to increase
traffic to the city

A phrase, so overused
A phrase ,without
credibility
A phrase, soo powerful
Soo powerful, that got us to
the city

The city , we love

The city , dreams maker
The city , dreams wrecker
The city , so brutal

The city, dreams wrecker
Dreams wrecker, like a
tornado storm
A storm , we all rush into
Because, the city has
opportunities

Dreams wrecker, like a
tornado storm
A storm, on s stopwatch

Stopwatch, is life
Life ,wasted in the city

A storm, we all rush into
Because, we are made to
believe
Belief , that the city has
opportunities
Opportunities, without
godfathers

The city , we love
The city , dreams maker
The city , dreams wrecker
The city , so brutal

12.FAILURE

Failure , what is it ?
Failure , how is it ?
Failure , so painful
Failure, can't be avoided

Failure , what is it
Failure , is nothing
Failure , is a lesson
Failure , is what you make it

Failure , is nothing
Nothing , to hurt yourself
over

Nothing , to risk your health over
Nothing , worth sleepless nights

Failure , is a lesson
A lesson , worth learning
A lesson , worth remembering
A lesson , worth teaching

Failure , what is it ?
Failure , how is it ?

Failure , so painful
Failure, can't be avoided

Failure , how is it
Failure , is painful
Failure , is energy draining
Failure , is the road to
success

Failure , is painful

So painful , that it gives us
sleeplessness
So painful, that we learn
from it We learn , to avoid
it

Failure , is the road to
success
A road , too thorny
That a few , can withstand
That's why , failure is
important

Failure , what is it ?

Failure , how is it ?
Failure , so painful
Failure, can't be avoided

Failure, so painful
Painful, that we always
remember
Remember, thus don't
repeat it
Reacting , means we didn't
learn

Painful , that we always
remember
Memories, to help us
Help us , to be better
So better , than our
previous selfs

Failure , what is it ?
Failure , how is it ?
Failure , so painful
Failure, can't be avoided

13.REJECTION

Rejection, hurts
Rejection , motivates
Rejection , scars
Rejection , teaches

Rejection , hurts
Hurts , so much
So much , that you cry
Tears , of healing

Hurts , so much

Hurts , like nothing else
Hurts , over time
Time. , heals the hurt

So much , that you cry
So much , that you hate
Hate , the feeling
Feeling , of rejection

Rejection, hurts
Rejection , motivates
Rejection , scars
Rejection , teaches

Rejection ,motivates
Motivates , you to be better
Better , than you were
Better , to society

Motivates, you to be better
Motivates, you to heal
Motivates, you to forgive
Motivates , you to learn

Better , to society

Better , to yourself
Better ,to others
Better , is good

Rejection, hurts
Rejection , motivates
Rejection , scars
Rejection , teaches

Rejection , scars
Scars , that heal
Scars , that remind
Remind us , that rejection
is normal
Scars , that heal

Heal , over time
Time , is the best consoler
Consoles , the soul

Rejection, teaches
Teaches , us of the past
mistakes
Prepares us , for the
unforeseen future
A future, where we help
other heal

Rejection, hurts
Rejection , motivates

Rejection , scars
Rejection , teaches

14.RACISM

Racism , is everywhere
Racism, ruins everything
Racism, is wrong
Racism, racism, why racism?

Racism , is everywhere
Everywhere ,in education

Everywhere , in healthcare
Everywhere ,in politics

Everywhere ,in education
Education , that doesn't
inspire
Education , that dims the
light
A light , of curiosity

Education, that doesn't
inspire
Education , full of white lies

Education , full of
misinformation
Education, should enlighten

Racism , is everywhere
Racism, ruins everything
Racism, is wrong
Racism, racism, why
racism?

Racism , ruins everything
Ruins everything ,
everywhere and anywhere
Ruins everything, that's
great and better

Ruins everything , in society

Ruins everything ,
everywhere and anything
Everywhere, it is
entertained
Anything, that entertains it
Racism, is poisonous

Racism ,is poisonous
So poisonous, like expired
poison
Poisonous, to everyone

Everyone, that entertains it

Racism , is everywhere
Racism, ruins everything
Racism, is wrong
Racism, racism, why
racism?

Racism, is wrong
No justification, for it
No entertaining , it
Racism ,is hate

Hate , instead of love
Love , that should be shared
Hate , unjustified
Hate , not needed

Racism , is everywhere
Racism, ruins everything
Racism, is wrong
Racism, racism, why
racism?